Bridges

Contents

Why Build Bridges?

Humans have used bridges throughout history. Bridges cross rivers, valleys, roads, and even parts of oceans. They provide crossings for people and animals as well as crossings for heavy road or rail traffic.

footbridge

rail bridge

People first built bridges so they could cross over rivers and creeks safely. They may have cut down a tree so that it fell across a river. They may have laid stepping-stones across a shallow river and laid timber or other stones on top to create a bridge.

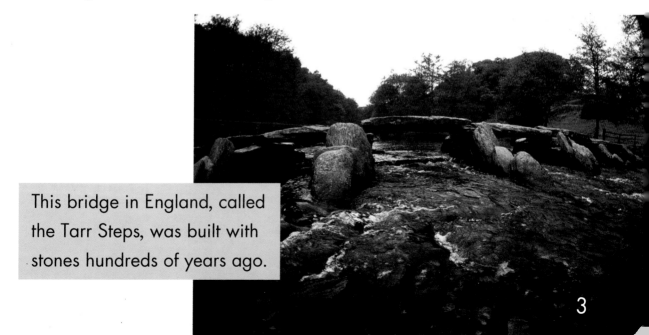

This bridge in England, called the Tarr Steps, was built with stones hundreds of years ago.

Hundreds of years ago, the Inca people built a bridge similar to this one over the Apurimac River in Peru. Today, local people maintain this bridge using traditional methods.

People used materials that they found nearby to build bridges. They used natural materials such as logs, tree branches, and ropes made from braided grasses and vines.

Building any type of bridge takes careful planning. What is the best location for the bridge? What will it need to support? How long will it be? Will it be strong enough to survive bad weather? What will be the best materials and design to use?

road bridge

A bridge needs to be able to support its own weight plus the weight of the many vehicles and people that pass over it. The flat part of a bridge used for crossing is called the **deck**.

5

Beam Bridges

One common type of bridge is called a **beam bridge**. A log across a creek is a simple beam bridge held up by the ground at each end.

Beam bridges are simple to build and are useful for crossing short distances.

Sometimes a beam bridge is held up by **piers**. The distance between two piers is called a **span**. To cross long distances, more piers can be built so that each span is short.

beam

pier

span

About two hundred years ago, people began to use iron, and later steel, to build bridges. The bridges built of iron or steel could stand up to weather better than wooden bridges.

About the same time, people started to travel by train. Trains needed to cross rivers, so many rail bridges were built. These rail bridges were often beam bridges with many piers. The piers often stood in riverbeds.

The piers sometimes got in the way of boats traveling beneath these bridges. They also were not always sturdy enough to survive stormy weather and rushing floods.

The original Tay Bridge in Scotland was nearly two miles long and had 85 spans. Less than two years after it was built, it collapsed during a storm.

Arch Bridges

Arch bridges are very strong. The shape of the arch gives these bridges their strength.

The shape of the arch takes weight from above and distributes it outward and downward toward the sides.

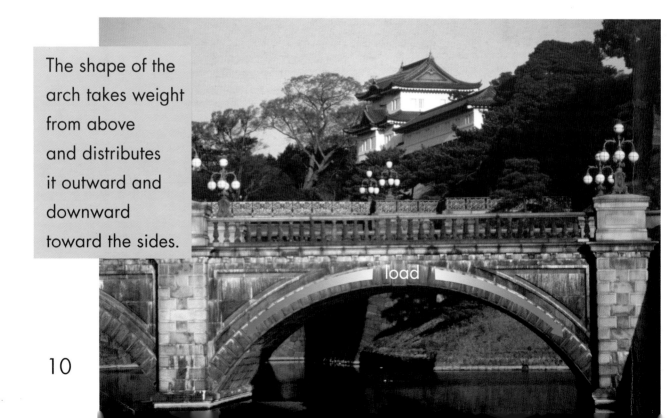

load

The Alcantara Bridge in Spain was built by the Romans in AD 105. It is still used today.

More than 2,000 years ago, the Romans built arch bridges and water pipe systems called **aqueducts**. Many Roman structures still stand, and people still use some of their bridges today.

Modern arch bridges are often made of steel or concrete. A steel arch is much lighter than a solid stone arch.

Australia's Sydney Harbour Bridge was constructed with steel. It was completed in 1932. Before the bridge was built, people had to cross the harbor by ferry, or they had to drive many miles to reach the other side. After the bridge was built, people and goods could be moved across the harbor much more quickly.

Look how the roadway of the Sydney Harbour Bridge hangs from its arch. In the bridge below, the roadway is on top of its arches.

The elegant Natchez Trace Parkway Bridge, built in 1994 in Tennessee, uses concrete for the arch and roadway.

13

Cantilever Bridges

A **cantilever bridge** is a special kind of beam bridge. Each section of the bridge is a beam balanced on a pier. The weight of the bridge on one side of the pier is balanced by the weight on the other side. Where two sections meet, they create tension that helps keep the bridge upright.

central span

piers

The Forth Bridge in Scotland, built in 1890, is one of the strongest bridges ever built.

A cantilever bridge is stronger than a simple beam bridge and can span greater distances. Many rail bridges are cantilever bridges because they must carry the weight of long, heavy trains.

Did You Know?

Tension works in bridges like it does in the game of tug-of-war: if two people with the same weight pull against each other, tension is created in the rope and nobody falls down.

Suspension Bridges

Suspension bridges can cross longer distances than beam, arch, or cantilever bridges. In a suspension bridge, strong lines called **cables** are strung from one side of the bridge to the other, usually over towers. The deck is suspended from these main cables.

San Francisco's Golden Gate Bridge

suspender cable

main cable

tower

main span

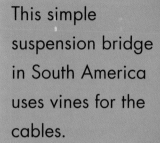

This simple suspension bridge in South America uses vines for the cables.

The cables in suspension bridges can be made of rope. Rope is not strong enough to carry much weight, however, and wet weather damages it. In modern bridges, cables are made of steel wire. This means that stronger and longer bridges can be built.

17

New York's Brooklyn Bridge, which opened in 1883, is one of the world's first great suspension bridges. Each of the main cables is about 16 inches (40 cm) in diameter and is made up of 5,282 steel wires.

The Brooklyn Bridge was built high enough to allow sailing ships with tall masts to travel underneath.

Cable-Stayed Bridges

Cable-stayed bridges are similar to suspension bridges, but the cables don't stretch from tower to tower. The deck hangs from cables attached directly to the towers instead.

tower

cable

deck

The Millau Viaduct is a cable-stayed bridge that crosses the valley of the river Tarn in France. It opened in December 2004. It has seven towers and is more than 8,000 feet (2,460 m) long.

The deck of the Millau Viaduct is about 886 feet (270 m) above the river — nearly as high as three Statues of Liberty stacked on top of one another.

Whether they are large or small, and whether they are made of stones or steel, bridges are useful all over the world.

Natchez Trace Parkway Bridge, USA

Tay and Forth Bridges, Scotland

Tarr Steps, England

Millau Viaduct, France

Brooklyn Bridge, USA

Golden Gate Bridge, USA

Alcantara Bridge, Spain

Apurimac River Bridge, Peru

Sydney Harbour Bridge, Australia

Glossary

aqueduct: A raised structure used to transport water.

arch bridge: A bridge strengthened by a curved structure.

beam bridge: A bridge supported at both ends by the ground or by piers.

cable: A strong, thick line, usually made of metal.

cable-stayed bridge: A bridge with a deck held up by cables attached to each side of a tower.

cantilever bridge: A bridge in which the deck (and supporting structure) on both sides of a pier balance each other.

deck: A roadway or platform. The part of a bridge that you cross.

pier: A support for one or more spans of a bridge.

span: The distance between two piers of a bridge.

suspension bridge: A bridge where the roadway is suspended (hung) from cables attached to supports at each end.